D0934108

Cross the Bridge to Life: Discover Your Adventure is a book that I believe many people will find helpful, including those that may have given up or lost hope. It is my desire that many will read this book and see the simple, understandable steps to take to have the adventurous life God desires to give them. I appreciate the fresh perspectives given in this book and I believe you will too.

—GARY CHAPMAN, AUTHOR OF
THE NEW YORK TIMES BEST-SELLER
THE FIVE LOVE LANGUAGES

Get ready to embark on a life-changing journey with my friend, Pastor David McGee. This book will get you off the bench of life and into…a God-filled adventure.

—STU EPPERSON JR., FOUNDER AND
OWNER OF TRUTH BROADCASTING
AND MEMBER OF THE
NRB BOARD OF DIRECTORS

Pastor David gets it! Being a Christian isn't just about attending church on Sunday morning, it's about being a Christian 24/7 in all areas of life. In *Cross the Bridge to Life* Pastor David teaches us how to "be the church." No matter where you are in your walk with God, you need to read this book.

—NATHAN TABOR, AUTHOR OF
BEAST ON THE EAST RIVER

Everyone has personal bridges to cross and obstacles on the road to success. David McGee has such a remarkable background and expertise, his insight will have a dramatic impact on your life decisions. This book is like a compass for living.

—PHIL COOKE, FILMMAKER AND
AUTHOR OF *BRANDING FAITH*

I have seen David minister and also share music and testimony. I believe he has a heart for the Lord…As David continues to allow the Lord to use him, I believe that God will continue to bless this man, his family, and ministry.

—Pastor Chuck Smith
Calvary Chapel, Costa Mesa, CA

God anointed the unique talents of David McGee and used them, against all odds, to create a significant gathering of his people in North Carolina and extend for great distances the missions reach of that gathering.

—Gayle D. Erwin, author of *The Jesus Style*

Cross the Bridge to Life should be the constant companion of every under-shepherd in the Savior's service. Most helpful is the fact that his emphasis is not only on methods, but more importantly on character, passion, and godliness. I read it twice and will continue to read it often to "regroup." I will share it with the entire leadership team as well as include it in our church.

—Pastor Ben Lawson
Calvary Chapel of the Sandhills

Pastor David McGee's *Cross the Bridge to Life* gets at the essence and substance of what it means to be authentically Christian. Instead of thinking in terms of "going to church" or being "churched" or "unchurched," Pastor David gets at what it really means to actually walk with Jesus day to day and in a very practical, real-world way. I know the man, am impressed by his ministry, and am pleased to commend his disciple-making book to you.

—Dr. Jeffrey L. Seif
Zola Levitt Ministries

cross *the* bridge *to* Life

DAVID McGEE

CREATION
HOUSE
A STRANG COMPANY

CROSS THE BRIDGE TO LIFE by David McGee
Published by Creation House
A Strang Company
600 Rinehart Road
Lake Mary, Florida 32746
www.strangbookgroup.com

Design Director: Bill Johnson
Cover design by Bill Johnson

Library of Congress Control Number: 2010921359
International Standard Book Number:
978-1-61638-160-8

First Edition

10 11 12 13 14 — 9 8 7 6 5 4 3 2 1
Printed in the United States of America

To God and His continuing work in my life and yours. To my family—Nora, Ashli and her husband John, John David, Benjamin Aaron—who have given and sacrificed much in the journey. To the reader, may you find this book worth the money paid for it and the time it takes to read it, and may you find the life that the God who gives life offers as we follow Him.

CONTENTS

ACKNOWLEDGMENTS

ALLOW ME TO thank the staff at Calvary Chapel of the Triad, who help me so much on a daily basis, and all of the individuals of the church who are committed in praying for me. Pastor Chuck Smith, thank you for giving me the opportunity to minister and for being the role model of a life poured out. To all of those at Creation House, thank you for helping bring this book to those who are holding it now.

INTRODUCTION

(Or, "Why I Wrote This Book")

I REALLY FELT LIKE the world needed another book, that somehow things would be incomplete without one more volume to put on your bookshelf.

Seriously, I think I can help you.

One of the great joys of being a pastor is that of helping others find their meaning, purpose, destiny, and calling in life. This book is simply an extension and expression of what God has called me to do and to be. When you picked up this book, you became potentially one of those I could help. If you glance through it and set it down now, it will perhaps only create questions, questions that you've probably been asking—whether out of interest or anguish—for years. If you do read it and think it through, taking some easy-to-understand steps, I will meet you on the other side. And, I can promise your life will be a better life, in simple exchange for the small cost and the time it took to read it. You will begin to see God do good things in your life.

This is not a self-help book, exhorting you to lift yourself by your bootstraps. Isn't that a weird saying? Imagine standing on the floor, grasping your own bootstraps, and attempting to lift yourself. It is impossible! Well, a lot of well-meaning people will offer advice that amounts to the same idea. So, self-help, no; this is a *God-help* book. The One who created you loves you, is for you, and wants you to live a more fruitful, joyful, and love-filled life. Ah, but perhaps nothing about that description of life appeals to you. That should trouble you, because it indicates that somewhere along the way you have lost the wonder of it all, the God-given joy of being alive. I am here to help you discover (or rediscover) that joy.

> And these things we write to you that your joy may be full.
>
> —1 JOHN 1:4, NKJV

You see, God is not merely concerned with providing fire insurance for your afterlife. He wants to give you a reason to live, a way to live, and the power to live. He wants to help you not just to exist but to live an extremely blessed and incredibly adventurous life.

This book is divided into chapters, because long ago someone decided that is how books should be done. But, then, we tend to divide our lives into chapters as well, don't we? I doubt if readers will see the chapter headings and think, "Awesome. This is what I have been looking for." But let me try to explain.

My father, who has completed life's journey and gone on before me, taught me the wonderful (and sometimes torturous) game of golf. He spent many hours teaching me. Some of those hours, to be honest, were very unnerving and painful. He constantly reminded me of the basics of the game. Whenever I ignored the basics, my game suffered, and my shots would reflect my disregard of those basics. But when I listened to my father, paid heed to those basics—head down, eye on the ball, etc.—then one of those magical moments might occur: the solid sound of the club striking the ball, the hissing sound it makes as it slices through the crisp morning air, that beautiful vision of the ball soaring against the blue sky, and the way it lands just as it is supposed to. Keep in mind, I have never had a whole game of moments like those, but it is such moments that have kept me playing.

Life is a lot like that. There are sand traps (the golf analogies will end with the Introduction, I promise), rough grass, and unforeseen or unavoidable hazards. But life can also contain those amazing, magic moments when everything comes together. Maybe you have forgotten what that was like, or maybe, sadly, those moments are few and far between. You see, my father was trying to teach me that it wasn't about the basics; it was about the game and the simple joy of playing. The basics simply help the golfer to play the game well. Sometimes we forget that and think the basics, the rules, are what life is all about. Not so, friend. That is the best path to the frustrating life of a Pharisee. The Pharisees of Jesus' day thought it was all about the rules. My intention in writing this book is to present the basics of the game of life without losing the God-given wonder of it all in the process.

I did not tell you the best part of playing golf with my father. It was not the solid contact I felt when I hit the ball. It was not its flight through the air. It was not the way or the place it landed. The best part was when I heard those words from my father, "Good shot, son." When we remember and respond to those basics, those principles, that our heavenly Father has given us regarding the game of life, it all comes together in an amazing and wonderful way, and we hear those words, "Well done."

May you discover through this book the wonder of a God-ordered life. Then, not only will you lead a better life but you will become a source of hope—dare I say, inspiration—to others to also live a better life. So, let's start our journey and walk together for a little while. I think you will find that instead of experiencing more rules and empty, broken promises, God's plan for your life will produce a fulfillment and a joy you have only dreamed of. This is not the promise of some guy writing a book; this is the promise of God Himself.

> My purpose is to give life in all its fullness.
>
> —JOHN 10:10, NLT

Let's take a walk. I think you'll find what you are looking for.

one

GO to CHURCH

"D O I HAVE to go to church?" No, you get to go to church.

I can hear the groans now. (There is a microphone hidden in the cover of this book.)

No, I am kidding. But you may think, "How could something this basic, something I gave up long ago, be part of the answer?" Perhaps you are one of those who is convinced that church is part of the problem. Please allow me to help you face that issue from God's perspective. God tells us the church is not part of the problem; the church is part of His solution.

> And let us not neglect our meeting together, as some people do, but encourage and warn each other, especially now

that the day of his coming back again is
drawing near.

—HEBREWS 10:25, NLT

My dad worked a lot, and he worked very hard.
It was only later in my life that I could understand,
much less appreciate, the sacrifices that he had made.
Early in the morning, when I would ask him, "Daddy,
do you have to go to work?" he would say, "No, son,
I get to go to work." He considered work a joy and
a privilege, and his attitude had a lot to do with his
enjoyment of it. So, do we have to go to church? No,
we get to go to church. Once again, our attitude deter-
mines to a large degree what we receive from church
and how much enjoyment we find in it.

I am not one who says everything is great in the
church today. There are lots of problems. There are
people who are in pulpits and on platforms because
it was a career choice instead of a calling, and to be
honest, their teaching shows it. I wish it were easy to
tell them apart, but sometimes, it is very easy to tell;
sometimes it is not. Of course, God always knows, but
He is not telling. So, yes, there are problems. There
is no such thing as the perfect church. If there were
such a thing, you could not join it, because none of

us is perfect. Once you or I joined that church, our own imperfections would defile it. Neither is there a perfect pastor. If you are looking for either one, you will live a life of frustration. You will find yourself swinging between joy when you think you have found it to sorrow when you realize you haven't, and the search continues. But there are good churches and good pastors out there. Sometimes it takes some searching to find them, but be encouraged. They are there, and they are worth looking for.

I would encourage you to look for a church home that teaches what our heavenly Father has already spoken to us through His Word. In fact, I think that some of the best churches offer a verse-by-verse, chapter-by-chapter approach, because we cannot improve on what God has already said. We just need to sort through it and figure out how it applies to our lives. This disciplined approach to the Bible helps us avoid the favorite topics that pastors (and their congregations) so often tend to camp around, and it adds balance.

⁓

You hear this excuse often: "Well, I had a bad experience in church." Hasn't everybody? Seriously, this one, very common response is hurting many people. I hope you are not adding to the confusion and pain in your life by disregarding God's plan for you. God is the one who came up with the idea of the church of brothers and sisters meeting together. I have found whenever I try to second-guess God, I end up being wrong.

What if we compared our thoughts on church to other, regular activities? For example, what if we treated going to church like soap? Both help us to see ourselves clearly and are for our benefit (and that of the people around us). What if we took those excuses that we use to avoid going to church and applied them to bathing?

- I was forced to bathe as a child.
- People who make soap are only after your money.
- I wash on special occasions like Christmas and Easter, and that's enough.
- People who wash are hypocrites; they think they are cleaner than everyone else.

- There are so many different kinds of soap; I can't decide which one is best.
- I used to wash, but it got boring. So, I stopped.
- None of my friends wash.
- The bathroom is never warm enough in the winter or cool enough in the summer.
- I'll start washing when I get older and dirtier.
- I can't spare the time.
- Soap irritates me sometimes.

These excuses to avoid bathing seem really lame, don't they? To be honest, they don't hold much water when it comes to church. Our excuses for avoiding church are just as silly.

OK, let's apply some of these same reasons and excuses to another area of our lives.

- I had a bad experience one time at work, so I gave up working.
- My boss ran over his allotted scheduled time, so I decided not to go back.

- I didn't get paid as much as I thought I would, so I decided it was not worth the effort to work.
- I once met someone at work I did not like, so I quit.

This sort of "logic" just doesn't work. How about this one?

- I've had bad experiences at restaurants, so I quit going out to eat. In fact, I quit eating altogether.

Wow! We wouldn't last long thinking like that. Now, let me reveal a couple of things about myself to you.

I am a *foodie*. A foodie is someone who is really into food. I love restaurants, and not just fancy restaurants. Over the years I have had many bad experiences in restaurants (and in churches). I have suffered from poor service, bad service, uncaring people, lukewarm food, bad food, and actually, on rare occasions, from poisonous food. In spite of that, I have not given up eating, nor have I given up going to restaurants. Why? Because when a restaurant experience *does* come together with great food, great service, and incredible atmosphere and surroundings, the effect is magical. I also have to realize I am not there as a food critic (though, being a foodie, I may tend to play the part). I am there to enjoy the food. When all these elements converge in a dining experience, it creates a lasting impression, an indelible memory. When it goes well, it is a memory that will last forever.

When I think about it, I have suffered similar experiences in churches as well. I have suffered from the experience of poor service when the sound, lighting, building, or the grounds were not being cared for. I have even experienced people that either did not care or actually seemed mad or disturbed that I was there, not to mention that I would dare to ask them for directions or for information. Sometimes the Word of God, our spiritual food, was served up lukewarm, with no passion or conviction or relevance to my life. Sometimes it was poisoned with human wisdom or, on rare occasions, with religious hypocrisy and spiritual pride. There are some churches (as well as some restaurants) that I will never return to. But for all that, when things do come together well in a church meeting, it is one of the most incredible and life-changing experiences we can have on this earth.

I am not saying that every aspect of the service has

to be perfect. But when it all comes together right, it is more than memorable. It is life-changing and forever alters the way I see God, myself, and those around me. Some of the worst people I ever met, I met in churches, but I have also met some of the best people in church too. And, I met my favorite person, Jesus, in a church service.

Whatever your perspective is on this issue, it is clear in Scripture that God's purpose is to reveal Himself in and through the church. Consider this passage:

> Unto him be glory in the church by Christ
> Jesus throughout all ages, world without
> end. Amen.
>
> —EPHESIANS 3:21, KJV

We're not talking about a building or denomination here. By *church* we mean the assembling together of God's people for the purpose of knowing and showing who He is.

Obviously, then, it would be accurate to say that more people meet God in church than meet Him outside of it. More people begin and grow in their relationship with God inside the church than outside of it. More people worship God in the church than outside of it. Where would the world be without the help, food, shelter, and aid the church has offered in times of trouble? In recent years, the church has expressed God's heart to the world during hurricanes, tsunamis, earthquakes, famines, and in response to the AIDS epidemic. God desires to express His heart to the world through the church.

Many people right now are growing in their understanding of God and of how much He loves them, and they are learning to love God more. Many of these people have had bad experiences, but somehow they were able to see the benefit and blessing of God's plan. Nothing is so simple and yet so rewarding as assembling with God's people, His church. It pays huge benefits for such a small investment of time. It is God's plan and purpose for us.

Don't wait for the hearse to take you to church in a casket. God would much prefer you to come while you are still alive. When you give up your search for the perfect church and look instead for a good church, you will find it. When you give up being a church hopper, bopper, and shopper and decide to grow where God wants you to be planted, you will bloom. Come discover the magic of being in the right church. You will be blessed, joyful, and happy you did. Don't give up on church; God is not giving up on you—even though He has had "bad experiences" with each of us.

two

BE the CHURCH

How can you be the church? The church was never supposed to be a group of buildings but a group of people. The church is the community of faith consisting of the followers of Jesus. If we are following Jesus, then how we look at the church tells a lot about us. If we focus mainly on finances in our description of the church, we should ask ourselves, Are we overly concerned with finances? If we say the church does not reach out to nonbelievers, are we reaching out to nonbelievers? If we say the church is cold, do we express warmth to those who visit our church or to the people we run into in our daily lives?

Churchgoers and non-churchgoers alike have asked me why the church does this or that. They use the pronouns *you* or *they*. They'll ask, "Why do *you* do this?" or "Why do *you* do that?" In talking with someone else, they may ask why *they* (the church) do this or that. This is a subtle indication that they do not consider themselves part of this community. It seems like a small thing, but when they begin changing, distancing themselves from their brothers and sisters, it becomes a big thing. When someone asks, "Why do *we* do this?" or "Why do *we* believe this?" it shows they recognize they are a part of something much larger than themselves.

Each of us has a longing in our heart and soul to be part of something larger than ourselves. We long for something that will last longer than a few days, years, or even a few decades. We want to be a part of something that will last forever, something eternal. God has placed a longing in each of us to be a part of that "something eternal," to be a member of His church, a member of the body of His Son, Jesus.

> And He [God] put all things under His [Jesus'] feet, and gave Him to be head over all things to the church, which is His body, the fullness of Him who fills all in all.
> —EPHESIANS 1:22–23, NKJV

We may try to satisfy that longing in various ways, but God's plan is for us to learn to find the fulfillment of that longing in a local community of believers.

Part of us wants to be part of the body of Christ.

We should be part of the body of Christ.

Part of a community of believers.

Part of Jesus.

Let's continue our walk.

three

BE the CHURCH—KNOW GOD

KNOW GOD? How can we possibly know God? The pictures in our minds are often of a secret society where the truths are dark, esoteric, and closely guarded. "You can't go in there; that is the Room of Secrets." I often encounter people who have bought into this idea of Christianity. They might say, "Well, I can't just *read* the Bible; I would get confused." The Bible is a book of massive complexities and profound philosophies. People of great intellect and education have been challenged and humbled by its depths. But it is also simple enough to change the life of anyone who dares read it and apply the truths it contains.

God wants to reveal Himself to us. He is not hiding on a mountain peak like the stereotypical, wizened guru who withholds his truths from all but the most dedicated, religious zealots. God has proclaimed His truths from the housetops. In every continent and in a multitude of languages, God has revealed Himself through His written Word. He wants us to know more about Him. He is not hiding in a hallway filled with secret passages. He desires a relationship with us. He is not only willing to tell us more about Himself but has already done so.

> In the last day, that great day of the feast, Jesus stood and cried, saying, If any man thirst, let him come unto me, and drink.
> —JOHN 7:37, KJV

Jesus is willing to reveal Himself to anyone who is willing to listen. He is not impressed with those who merely dress right, act right, who have it "on the ball," who appear to have everything going for them. No, actually, He seems to go out of His way to find those who society has deemed unworthy—the unattractive, the unsuccessful, and the unlovable, those who do not act right or dress right.

> But God has chosen the foolish things of the world to put to shame the wise, and God has chosen the weak things of the

world to put to shame the things which
are mighty.

—1 Corinthians 1:27, nkjv

So God wants to talk and has spoken. The question
is, Are we willing to listen?

If the mayor of the town you live in, the governor
of your state, or the president of the United States
called you, I think you would take the time to listen
and see what he or she had to say. Should we not offer
the same courtesy to God? Many who reject Christianity have not really taken the time to adequately
explore its claims. Many have rejected it after a high-altitude flyover, if you will. That is like flying over Los
Angeles and deciding you don't like it. Don't like it?
You have never been in it. You have only flown over
it. Until you walk its streets, taste its incredible foods,
meet its colorful people, and experience its unique
weather, you really won't know if you like it or not.
You have to get to know it before you can make that
judgment. How many foods have you thought were
horrible before you actually tasted them? How many
movies have you rejected by title alone? Then later
you actually watched the movie, and it became one
of your favorites.

Christianity has never been particularly fashion-able. In some circles, people have rejected Christianity, never having adequately examined it. It is kind of like the way guys always act like we don't like chick flicks. Some really are way too mushy to even carry a reasonable story line. (Come on, girls.) So around our guy friends, we act like all chick flicks are silly. The problem is, you would miss out on a lot of good movies—OK, at least some good movies—if you wrote off all chick flicks. You could miss out on a couple of hours of enjoyable entertainment and perhaps some truth that would change the way you look at things. Similarly, if you write off God without fully examining the truths He is so willing to share with us, you will miss out on much more than a just a few hours of entertainment.

Take a look at this verse. Jesus is revealing Himself to anyone willing to listen.

> Take my yoke upon you. *Let me teach you,*
> because I am humble and gentle, and you
> will find rest for your souls.
> —MATTHEW 11:29, NLT, EMPHASIS ADDED

Sounds incredible, doesn't it? I am amazed that people say the Bible and Christianity are not relevant. How can the offer of peace and rest be irrelevant in this crazy, hectic, cell phone, iPod world we live in? So, Jesus offers us peace and offers to teach us a better way to live. Not relevant?

> The thief's purpose is to steal and kill and destroy. My purpose is to give life in all its fullness.
>
> —John 10:10, NLT

So the questions are, How do we get to know this God? and, How can we participate in these promises of peace, rest, and fullness? The answer to one is the answer to the other. When we get to know God, we can also take part in these promises of peace and rest. So what keeps us from this? What obstructs us from knowing God and experiencing His *shalom*?

Shalom is much more than peace. According to *Strong's Concordance*, it means "safe, well, happy, friendly, health, prosperity, peace." Now there's a list that appeals to no one, right? I think all of those things appeal to all of us. Who can honestly say they're not interested? We all long to be able to use these words to describe our lives. What is the problem? The heart of the human problem is the problem of the human heart. What causes the unrest is also what separates us from God. How ironic it is that the very thing that alienates us from God, that steals the peace and rest He longs to give us, is what moved Him to die for us. He desired that our relationship with Him might be restored. Let me explain.

There is this problem of our wrongdoing. In some circles, people think it is enough to recognize it and feel bad about it. In some teachings, the entire goal is to make you feel bad. While it is important to recognize there is a problem, the goal of God is not just to make you feel bad about the problems you have; His desire is to lead you to the solution.

> When he heard this, Jesus replied, "Healthy people don't need a doctor—sick people do." Then he added, "Now go and learn the meaning of this Scripture: 'I want you to be merciful; I don't want your sacrifices.' For I have come to call sinners, not those who think they are already good enough."
> —MATTHEW 9:12–13, NLT

So, the fact that you have this awareness that there is a problem is actually not the problem but can be part of the solution. Way too many people, Christian or not, think the goal is for us to feel bad. God's desire is that the pain, shame, guilt, or depression that we experience from realizing we have trashed our lives would lead us to the right response.

> The Lord is not slow to do what he has promised, as some think. Instead, he is patient with you, because he does not want anyone to be destroyed, but wants all to turn away from their sins.
> —2 PETER 3:9, TEV

God does not want us to try to fix ourselves but to simply agree with Him regarding the nature of the problem. (The truth is, He has already taken care of the problem.) You cannot argue with the fact that you have done wrong things. You simply can't. Everyone has done wrong things—everyone, including myself, the apostle Paul, Billy Graham, and every other preacher, pastor, and minister throughout history. Every person who has ever lived, churchgoer or not, has done wrong (Jesus, of course, being the only exception). That is the cause of our unrest, our lack of peace, and our sense of being distanced from God. It's sort of like when you have an argument with someone you are close to and then feel hesitant to contact them afterward.

When I was a young boy, I often would break my toys playing too hard with them. At that point I had a decision to make. My dad was a mechanical and aeronautical engineer, so there wasn't anything he could not fix (or replace, if needed). So, anytime I would break a toy, I would just bury the toy in the toy bin and act like it wasn't a problem, but the problem was still there. I could act like nothing was wrong, but deep down, even if no one else knew it, I knew my toy was broken, and I was haunted by that knowledge. Occasionally, I would look into the toy bin and see it. Instead of going to my father for help, I tried to hide my problem, but it was still there. Perhaps it was the shame and guilt of breaking the toy my father had given me. Perhaps I knew I had not used the toy the way Dad said I should. Sometimes, I knew I was responsible for breaking it. Funny, Dad did not usually try to assign blame. He seemed more interested in fixing what was broken.

The alternative to that strategy of trying to hide my broken toy was simply to go to my dad and ask his help, knowing that he could fix anything I brought him. I would take it to my father, knowing that my daddy could fix anything. Your spiritual Father, your heavenly Daddy, can fix anything, including your broken life, your broken heart, and your broken dreams. Don't try to hide the broken parts of your life. Bring them to Him in confidence, knowing that He can fix anything.

Did you ever see *Rudolph the Red-nosed Reindeer*? Many of us grew up watching that Christmas program each year. Anyone who would get offended about my mentioning Rudolph is reading the wrong book (but probably would have put it down long ago anyway). In the TV show, there was a place called The Island of Misfit Toys. Toys that had some design flaw or had become broken or worn out were sent to this island. To be clear, it is not God's intention that any of us should be born with a design flaw. But wrong human choices, wrong human thinking, and wrong human action have perverted the world God gave us. As a result we all suffer things that God never intended for us to suffer. God gave each of us a free will so we could choose to love Him. Because of our misuse of that freedom, we find ourselves on "a planet of lost toys." All of us have made wrong choices. Some of us have suffered further breaking by the choices of those around us. But here's the good news: someone much better than Santa or Rudolph has come to us and offered to help fix us. The very One who created us has diagnosed the problem, has formulated a solution, and has (already) come to our little island (or our little planet) to fix what is wrong.

His solution was to pay the price for all of our wrongdoing. The only perfect person to ever walk this planet volunteered to die in our place, the perfect for the imperfect. That is what Jesus did for us on the cross. If you think you have done no wrong, that is what will keep you from asking Him for forgiveness. If you know that you have done wrong, then that realization should not drive you away from Him but to Him. Perhaps you can fool people into thinking you don't have any problems, but God knows not only the list of all your problems but also the complete history of your life.

Our wrongdoing created a vast canyon that separated us from God. There was a gaping chasm that we could not jump across, even though we may have tried our hardest. Some people think that by being good enough they can bridge that gap. But how good is "good enough" before a God who is perfect? You might as well try to jump over the Grand Canyon. So the solution is not to try harder. We cannot fix the problem; we can only acknowledge it. God has the solution. He built a bridge over that gap, and the bridge is called the cross.

The cross.

The bridge.

The bridge is the cross.

We need to cross this bridge.

> He canceled the record that contained the charges against us. He took it and destroyed it by nailing it to Christ's cross.
> —COLOSSIANS 2:14, NLT

All right, so then, problem solved right? Well, almost. We have the diagnosis of the problem from the doctor. We have the right prescription for the problem from the pharmacist. Now comes our part. It's really a small part and so simple and straightforward. Our part is to accept that Jesus died not just for the whole world but for each one of us individually. Once we get a glimpse of the magnitude of God's love for us, our hearts can only respond by asking Him

31

to forgive us of our sins and to give us the power to live for Him. How do you do this? By praying. What is praying? It is simply talking to God. If you want to be forgiven, just pray the following prayer, or one like it, out loud.

> *Dear God,*
>
> *I believe You died for me so that I could be forgiven of my sins. I believe You were raised from the dead so that I could walk in a new way of life. I have done wrong, and I am sorry. Please forgive me for all the wrong things I have done. Please give me the power to live for You all the rest of my life. In Jesus' name, amen.*

Do not turn back to the problem now, but develop your relationship with God. As you turn more toward Him, you will be turning away from your sins and wrongdoing. Your life will change as you never thought possible. You just made the greatest decision you can ever make in life.

Congratulations, and welcome to a better life!

four

BE the CHURCH—LEARN ABOUT GOD and the BIBLE

CHECK OUT THE following quote by Robert Chapman:

The Bible contains the mind of God, the state of man, the way of salvation, the doom of sinners, and the happiness of believers. Its doctrines are holy, its precepts are binding, its histories are true, and its decisions are immutable. Read it to be wise, believe it to be safe, and practice it to be holy. It contains light to direct you, food to support you, and comfort to cheer you.

It is the traveler's map, the pilgrim's staff, the pilot's compass, the soldier's sword, and the Christian's charter. Here Paradise is restored, Heaven opened, and the gates of hell disclosed. Christ is its grand subject, our good the design, and the glory of God its end.

It should fill the memory, rule the heart, and guide the feet. Read it slowly, frequently, and prayerfully. It is a mine of wealth, a paradise of glory, and a river of pleasure. It is given you in life, will be opened at the judgment, and be remembered forever. It involves the highest responsibility, will reward the greatest labor, and will condemn all who trifle with its sacred contents.[1]

Whether you agree with every part of that quote or not, the Bible is worthy of our attention, study, and respect. I have read many books, and none were as life changing or rewarding as the Bible.

This chapter title is "Be the Church—Learn About God and the Bible." Ideally, learning about one should involve learning about the other. If you try to learn about God without the Bible, you become subject to whims, impressions, and emotions that could mislead you in your inquiries. If you try to learn about the Bible without learning about God, it becomes a dry, academic exercise. God points to His Word, and His Word points to Him. As you get to know the Word of God, you will get to know the God of the Word.

Why not get to know the Bible? If there is even a chance the Bible is what it claims to be, why not take the time to dig in and check it out? Here are some of the reasons and excuses people give. Let's deal with them, one at a time.

1. Because it was written so long ago, the Bible is no longer relevant.

Well, it was written a long time ago. And it is true the world has changed a lot. Instead of walking or riding horses, we now travel in cars and planes. The way we travel has changed, but the concept hasn't. Instead of talking face-to-face, using handwritten documents, and drawing pictures, we now use computers, cell phones, e-mail, text messaging, and blogs. The way we communicate has changed, but not the concept itself. We still desire to communicate with each other. What about the big things in life: birth, life, death, anger, love, hope, joy, laughter, pain, suffering—have any of those things changed? No. Has the fact that we experience emotions changed?

No, again. We may think we understand them better now, but they have not changed. The Bible still deals with human experience, emotions, and spirituality and speaks to those issues today as accurately as it did many generations ago.

Some will say older books are no longer relevant, but how old is too old? If we exclude older works of literature, where will the historical cut-off be, and who is worthy to make such a judgment? If we set the cut-off at twenty-five hundred years before present day, we've just wiped out all the Greek writers of philosophy and drama. Set it at one thousand years, and we lose *Beowulf*, Chaucer, the Magna Carta, and numerous other significant writings. Five hundred years ago? We've just ripped Shakespeare and a huge slice of English literature and culture right out of history. Ouch! Three hundred years ago? Well, now we've lost the Bill of Rights and the Declaration of Independence. Not sure how we will run the U.S. without those things, but you get the point. *Older* doesn't necessarily mean "irrelevant" and "useless."

2. The Bible is filled with contradictions.

This is one of those sayings that after years of repetition, people have come to believe it to be the truth. Whenever I hear someone say this, I offer them my Bible and say, "Really? Will you please show me one?"

I have never, repeat *never*, had anyone point one out.

Far too often, people believe this excuse without checking it out for themselves. That's amazing, especially when you consider how often we hear people accuse Christians of just believing things without checking out the facts. In all honesty, there are some things that are a little confusing about the Hebrew numbering system, for example, that scholars are still figuring out, but that hardly constitutes a contradiction. We often speak in apparent contradictory terms. We may say of the same person, "I love her," or "I hate her," depending on the situation. "I like the hot weather," or "I like the cold weather." "I like the rain," or "I like the sunshine." These are situational contradictions. You may say, "I am really hungry," in the afternoon, but after a big meal, "I am really full." Well, which is it? Are you contradicting yourself? No, you are simply reporting a change in the state of your hunger; there is no contradiction.

3. The Bible is so confusing.

Well, a book of the scope and magnitude of the Bible can be overwhelming. But it really is not all that confusing. Young children can hear the story of the prodigal son and learn something from it, yet a scholar can read it a hundred times and see new aspects and applications every time. Adam making the wrong choice in the Garden of Eden reflects typical human nature, yet it is immense in its implications and effects. There are more difficult passages in the Bible, but they usually have less to do with practical personal application. Loving God and loving people, again, is easily understood by a small child. As Mark Twain once said, "It is not the part of the Bible I don't understand that bothers me."[2] For all of its complexities, that is hardly a reason to write the Bible off. How many of us have a complete understanding of the technology behind computers or television or even automobiles? But we don't let that stop us from taking advantage of their benefits. There are so many places to get help to understand the Bible. You can start at www.crossthebridge.com to learn more.

4. The Bible was written by man.

Well, I do believe the Bible was inspired by God, but for a moment let's say that it was written only by men and that they were not inspired by God. Is there any other book that has benefited humanity, been a positive influence on culture, encouraged freedom for slaves, or moved people to love one another and reach out to those in need more than this book? No. Is there any other book we dismiss with a wave of our hand and say with our noses in the air that we won't read because it was written by man? To say that is to write off every book that has ever been written since the dawn of time. Doesn't make sense, does it? It's like saying, "I won't read that, because it was written on a computer." God used man as His writing instruments, much like we use pens, pencils, and computers to write things.

5. The Bible is dull and boring.

What? Without God's help, we may not understand its mysteries, but to read of the life of Jesus, for example, is anything but boring. I think this complaint may have come from people sitting under the ministries of boring teachers. When those professing to be teachers take a book that is filled with so much enjoyable, incredible, supernatural stuff, and turn it into a boring academic exercise, that really is sad and tragic.

6. There are so many different versions of the Bible.

Yes, there are. There are paraphrases and translations. A translation brings the meaning from one language to another, whereas a paraphrase is usually a rewording of a document within the same language. But when we say *version*, we think of things like updates that make the original or earlier version obsolete. No, that definition doesn't apply here. The word *version* can also mean a different version, as in a different version of the story or of the truth, coming from a different source. No, that doesn't work here either. There are translations, which I prefer, and paraphrases. All are derived from the same basic source documents. Portions of those documents date back to A.D. 125 for the New Testament (the Ryland documents) and as far back as 300 B.C. for the Old Testament (the Dead Sea scrolls). Ask your pastor to recommend a translation for you, or contact us; we'll be glad to make some recommendations, but don't let that excuse keep you from enjoying the Bible.

I am hoping that by now you've allowed me to persuade you to get to know God and the Bible. You may be asking, "How do I do it?" I want to help you with this. You are not alone. We have many free materials available at www.crossthebridge.com. There are CDs, DVDs, and podcasts that are also available. There is a link that will take you to the online site of the church where I pastor and teach. There you can access resources and teachings that will walk you, verse by verse, through the Bible. Another helpful website for personal study is www.blueletterbible. org. Find a church where the pastor actually reads and teaches from the Bible itself, rather than merely preaching his opinions and speculations regarding Scripture.

I am amazed by Christians who don't know what they believe and why. They haven't taken the time to read and study the Bible. Considering how easy it is to find a scholarly translation of the Bible in our own contemporary language and how accessible helpful biblical resources are in our generation, it amazes me how scripturally illiterate our culture is. In less fortunate times and cultures, Christians have been willing to die in order to preserve and share the Word of God. Find a church that honors the Bible and demonstrates that by dedicating a large part of the service to its reading and teaching. Take the time to read, because Jesus took the time to bleed.

five

BE the CHURCH—LIVE for GOD

O K, "LIVE FOR God." What does that mean? What is the passion of your life? What is it that gets you up in the morning and keeps you up at night? Is it work, sports, a hobby, something else? God wants you to be passionate about Him, because that's how He feels about you. This is coming from someone who has lived for money, fame, glory, sex, drugs, rock 'n roll, alcohol...OK, OK, the list is longer, but you get the point. Whenever I lived for other things, I was living somewhere between misery and mere existence. God wants us to do more than just exist, and He tells us so.

> The thief's purpose is to steal and kill and destroy. My purpose is to give life in all its fullness.
>
> —JOHN 10:10, NLT

God, who gave us life, wants to teach us how to live. He is willing to share this incredible knowledge with us if we will just pause and listen.

So, how do we experience this incredibly abundant life filled with joy, love, peace, and contentment? Is it by getting out of debt, saving money, getting the best job, the best woman (or man, for you ladies), the nicest house, and the fastest car? Is that how we live the best life? Or is there a better way?

What on earth are we here on this earth for? Simply put, God has given us life to live for Him.

Not the house.

Not the cars.

Not the ladies or the men.

Not the job.

Listen to what Jesus says:

> He who finds his life will lose it, and he who loses his life for My sake will find it.
> —MATTHEW 10:39, NKJV

Here's another translation of the same verse.

> If you cling to your life, you will lose it; but if you give it up for me, you will find it.
> —MATTHEW 10:39, NLT

Do you know how many times this passage or verse occurs in the first four books of the New Testament? (These books, Matthew, Mark, Luke, and John, are called the Gospels, because they tell of the life and death of Jesus.) Obviously, it is in there once. Is it there twice? Yes. Three times? Yep, keep going. Four times? Is it in all four Gospels? Yep, keep going. Actually, it is in all four of the Gospels six times in all: Matthew 10:39, Matthew 16:25, Mark 8:35, Luke 9:24, Luke 17:33, and John 12:25. When Jesus repeats something that often, it is safe to assume He wants us to hear it, that it's important! I used to wonder why Jesus repeated Himself; then I had kids, and I found I was repeating myself all the time: "Don't do that," "Don't do that," "Don't do that." (Yes, I am sure it is only *my* children that need that.) He repeats Himself to teach us, because we need to be reminded. When Jesus repeats something so many times, it's an indication that the concept must be very important, something necessary for our spiritual well-being.

God wants us to enjoy our lives. He designed us, and He knows better than anyone what we need to be happy. Giving up your life for Him will involve, among other things, laying aside your own interests for the sake of others. Secular psychiatry is beginning to realize that a key to overcoming depression is to engage in intentional acts of kindness toward others. It would seem the secret is out. But are we listening?

Will God show us how to live for Him? Absolutely, and He already has. In this book I will continue to try to show the simple picture that is found within the pages of the most incredible book there is. Of course, I'm talking about the Bible.

The Lord doesn't just say, "OK, I died for you. You take it from here." No, He promises His help from here on out. Help for what? Help to get to church? Help to get though life with no pain? No, He gives us something much more precious. He helps you and keeps you through all the good times and the bad. You remember that passage in the marriage vows, "for better or for worse"? It's like that; God's made a covenant, an agreement with us. He doesn't say there won't be hard times, but He promises to keep you through those times. Some of the really tough times will help build your faith. Corrie ten Boom said, "You don't know Jesus is all you need until Jesus is all you've got."[1] The tough times will help you appreciate the good times. We can be assured that God is at work in our lives. He will not grow bored with us.

Being confident of this very thing, that He
who has begun a good work in you will
complete it until the day of Jesus Christ.
—PHILIPPIANS 1:6, NKJV

☙

God wants us to live for Him. What does that mean?
What does God mean when He says, "No other gods
before me"? Is it just that He is selfish? Absolutely not.
We were created to have a relationship with God. He
may feel jealous over us in the way a husband or wife
feels jealous over the affections of his or her spouse,
but that is something different. We were wired in such
a way that we need to put God first. Whenever we
put other things first, before God, things start going
haywire in our lives, even if those things are good
things. If we put our work before God (and work is
a good thing), it knocks us out of correct orienta-
tion, and our lives can go into a tailspin. If we put
our families before the Lord, then our families will
be out of whack.

We have to be careful with our priorities. As a
pastor, I have discovered that most people have their
priorities out of whack. They count their families,
their jobs, even their hobbies more important than

their relationship with God. At first glance you might think, "No, that is not right. I need to put my wife and children first. If I put God first, the other things will be out of whack." Well, take it from me. I'm a father of three children, a pastor, and a husband. I've found if I don't put God first over my family, my wife, my children, and my ministry, then everything will suffer because of my misplaced priorities. God knows that and tries to tell me in so many ways.

> You shall have no other gods before Me.
> —EXODUS 20:3, NKJV

> But seek first the kingdom of God and His righteousness, and all these things shall be added to you.
> —MATTHEW 6:33, NKJV

> And he will give you all you need from day to day if you live for him and make the Kingdom of God your primary concern.
> —MATTHEW 6:33, NLT

So, I mentioned some of the things that could get in the way of your relationship with God—some good, some not so good. What about money? Money is really, really evil, right? Doesn't the Bible say that it's the root of all evil? Here is what it actually says:

> For *the love of money* is at the root of all kinds of evil. And some people, craving money, have wandered from the faith and pierced themselves with many sorrows.
> —1 TIMOTHY 6:10, NLT, EMPHASIS ADDED

Money itself is not evil. Our love of money can cause us all kinds of problems, though, because we allow it to have such a strong influence over us. Reread that verse above.

How many times have you seen someone do something really unjust or immoral because they got caught up in the pursuit of money? You have to choose to either live for God or live for money and the materialism that follows it. I am not against followers of Jesus possessing nice things; I just don't think that things should possess followers of Jesus. Look at this one.

> No one can serve two masters. For you will hate one and love the other, or be devoted to one and despise the other. You cannot serve both God and money.
> —MATTHEW 6:24, NLT

It is like your life is a car that has to travel over dangerous terrain. You will need someone driving who knows the map and is a good driver. Who or what will you allow to take the driver's seat of your life? You have to choose God. You can choose life and blessings.

> Today, I have given you the choice between life and death, between blessings and curses. I call on heaven and earth to witness the choice you make. Oh, that you would choose life, that you and your descendants might live!
> —DEUTERONOMY 30:19, NLT

Or choose to serve something else: yourself, money, success. The list is long, but the result is the same.

> Now he who received seed among the thorns is he who hears the word, and the cares of this world and the deceitfulness of riches choke the word, and he becomes unfruitful.
> —MATTHEW 13:22, NKJV

Friend, please live for something more than just temporary, passing things. Live for something eternal, lasting, and permanent. If you don't, you will place yourself in what will end up to be a potentially dangerous and destructive way to live.

> Therefore whoever hears these sayings of Mine, and does them, I will liken him to a wise man who built his house on the rock: and the rain descended, the floods came, and the winds blew and beat on that house; and it did not fall, for it was founded on the rock. But everyone who hears these sayings of Mine, and does not do them, will be like a foolish man who built his house on the sand: and the rain descended, the floods came, and the winds blew and beat on that house; and it fell. And great was its fall.
>
> —MATTHEW 7:24–27, NKJV

Live for God. Then and only then, when—not if—the storms come, you will be just fine. You house will not fall.

Choose life. Choose blessing. Choose God.

51

six

BE the CHURCH—GIVE to GOD THROUGH the CHURCH

I SIMPLY COULD NOT write a book about following God and not mention finances. God wants to be involved with everything in our lives. It is hard to overestimate the important role finances play in our lives. I am not talking about whether or not we put too much emphasis on it. I have done that; we all have. We work to earn it, spend it at the store for food and other necessities. We trade our time for it, our energies, and our attention. No doubt about it, money plays an important role in our lives. The fact is that we can't give God control of our lives without giving Him control of our finances. That's the point. God is not poor. He does not need our money. But He knows that to have spiritually productive and balanced lives, we need His wisdom and input in all areas and perhaps especially in the realm of money.

What we spend time and money on shows where our priorities are. God gives us a plan that helps us live truly fruitful (the fruit of the Spirit is love, joy, peace, etc.) and balanced lives. We are all in danger of being too materialistic, greedy, and selfish. You only have to look at Wall Street (and probably your own local Main Street) to hear of people doing really horrible things in order to accumulate wealth. All of us are in danger of committing those acts if we are not careful. Most of these people, when they are caught, seem genuinely horrified at their acts, just as we are when we hear of them. I remember a scandal where a funeral home betrayed their customers' trust by mishandling bodies, cremating them and then reporting them buried. When they were caught and confronted, they tried to blame their actions on how competitive the business was and how hard it was to make a profit. When people are caught doing wrong, they always offer excuses, attempting to justify their choices and actions. We're all really good at that, shifting the blame off of ourselves and onto "extenuating circumstances." But God sees through all that. He sees that our selfishness needs help. He not only offers us help, but He gives us a plan. He has a plan that will lead us down a path of light instead of the dark path of greed and despair that the world offers. But be ready, it is radical.

⤚

It is more blessed to give than to receive.
—ACTS 20:35, NLT

I guess, like most people, I think of this verse more at Christmastime than any other. Jesus wired us to be a giving and generous people. There is this—cue the ominous organ music, and out of the shadows appears a man with a cape—darker side to us. We see both sides, sometimes, at Christmas. Have you ever watched people in a store around the holiday season? While they are shopping and cheerfully giving gifts to the ones they love, they are screaming, pushing, and being flat-out mean to others around them in order to get the best deals. No doubt about it, there are two natures in each of us. Which one do you want to rule in your life? I think most of us would say, "The generous one." We like to think of ourselves as generous people. While we may want to be generous, our actions don't always line up with our ideals. Though we may want to be generous and may see ourselves that way, statistics tell us this does not always line up with our actions.[1]

We gladly give 30 percent of our income or more to pay the mortgage or rent for the house we live in. Sometimes, we'll give more than 10 percent for a car payment. We often spend hundreds and even thousands on vacations. We justify these things with, "Well, we work hard, and we deserve it." But what about God, the One who has given us so much—our minds, our bodies, our loved ones, His forgiveness? What does He deserve? He deserves our lives, our commitment, and the recognition that all we have comes from Him. I don't think most people would argue with the fact that God *deserves* a tithe, or the first 10 percent of what we earn. The Bible does teach us that.

> You must set aside a tithe of your crops—one-tenth of all the crops you harvest each year. Bring this tithe to the place the LORD your God chooses for his name to be honored, and eat it there in his presence. This applies to your tithes of grain, new wine, olive oil, and the firstborn males

of your flocks and herds. The purpose of tithing is to teach you always to fear the LORD your God.

—DEUTERONOMY 14:22–23, NLT

How terrible it will be for you teachers of religious law and you Pharisees. Hypocrites! For you are careful to tithe even the tiniest part of your income, but you ignore the important things of the law—justice, mercy, and faith. You should tithe, yes, but you should not leave undone the more important things.

—MATTHEW 23:23, NLT

So, why don't more people—more born-again, Bible-believing people—tithe? We cannot find fault with God. The issue revolves around giving to a perfect God by paying tithes and offerings to an imperfect church. Let's talk about that.

We have all heard the stories about the preachers who make way too much. The TV, the Internet, the media in general, offer frequent stories covering this man or that woman who makes way too much in their work for the kingdom of God. A simple question: How many of those who make "way too much" are there?

Is it a few, a dozen, a few dozen? Newscasters seem preoccupied with those ministries, perhaps because they are in the public eye, and yet in reality they make up a very small percentage of all pastors. In my life, I have met hundreds and hundreds of pastors that don't make "way too much." As a matter of fact, you could easily argue they don't make enough. Many of these hard-working pastors cannot afford health insurance. Many have to work part-time jobs and sometimes even full-time jobs in addition to pastoring churches. In starting the church I now pastor, I did not draw a salary for a year and half while the church was being established. When God calls someone to ministry, those kinds of sacrifices are not unusual.

Many of these pastors work hard to serve people, people who, for the most part, are not tithing and giving. These folks may excuse their lack of giving by pointing to those few extreme examples of ministers who are paid too much. Their reluctance to give has no bearing on those ministries that they refer to, but, instead, it limits and even punishes the one ministry trying to help them where they attend. As my dad used to say, "Two wrongs don't make a right." It is a sad issue that these people don't always handle finances responsibly. The Bible encourages us to be givers, and someday we will stand before God and give an account for how we used the blessings He sent our way. I suspect that this excuse of overpaid ministers is nothing more than a smokescreen we use to mask our own stinginess.

Friend, if you have a problem with some of these people that "make too much" or "spend too much," then don't give to those ministries. Give to the church where you attend. Do not look for excuses not to give. The pastor of your church may make more than you or less than you depending on the church size, his responsibilities, and what your own occupation is.

You can always find an excuse not to give. You can never find a reason to relieve you of your Christian duty and calling of giving and being generous. God tells us to give. Not only does it finance the work of the kingdom of God, but it changes our hearts for the better.

The church at large, the body of Christ, is an incredible organism and organization. At our church, among other things, we help to feed the hungry, clothe those who are in need, and help people keep their heat on in the winter. We proclaim good news to those without hope, offer forgiveness to those trapped in shame and guilt, and show love to people who may not see it anywhere else. There are many churches involved in these things; helping during floods, hurricanes, and other natural disasters; and attempting to be a blessing and an expression of God's heart to a world starving for love. But this is not *why* we give.

Most charitable organizations ask you to give in order to help with needs outside of your home, family, and life. Tithing, though, is not God's way of raising money but of raising His children. He encourages us to give and be generous because it helps to slay the envy, greed, materialism, and selfishness in us that keeps us from becoming who we are called to be and, on some level, who we long to become. When we commit to tithing—I don't mean by giving from whatever is left at the end of the month, but by giving when we first receive our income (our *firstfruits*)—it changes us. We don't give God what's left, but we give to Him what is right. We show by that act that God is important to us. When we give with a generous and cheerful heart, we are giving away not only our money but our selfishness and materialism as well.

Often we are told that we need to give in order to get. While I have an issue with some of those teachers, there is truth underlying the statement. It's not as though by giving to God you will somehow be excused from having to be responsible with your finances and that you will miraculously emerge from your debt. But there is a sort of heavenly exchange that takes place, and God does delight in cheerful givers.

> Bring all the tithes into the storehouse so there will be enough food in my Temple. If you do," says the LORD Almighty, "I will open the windows of heaven for you. I will pour out a blessing so great you won't have enough room to take it in! Try it! Let me prove it to you! Your crops will be abundant, for I will guard them from insects and disease. Your grapes will not shrivel before they are ripe," says the LORD Almighty.
>
> —MALACHI 3:10–11, NLT

In one translation of this passage it reads, "I will rebuke the devourer for your sake" (KJV). Perhaps part of what giving does is to rebuke the devourer in us, that part of us that will lead us in a troubling quest for more, more, more. It's the same part of us that is never satisfied with what we have and always lusts for more. That ceaseless thirst for materialism has ruined many lives, and it will rule us unless we resist it by consistently responding to God's encouragement to give. We receive more in return than our money's worth (in terms of kingdom benefits) when we give from a cheerful and generous heart. We have traded wisely. For the sake of the kingdom, for the sake of your calling, and for the sake of protecting your loved ones by maintaining right kingdom priorities, give your tithe, or 10 percent, to the church.

seven

BE the CHURCH—LOVE GOD and LOVE PEOPLE

THIS IS A very basic and extremely challenging statement:

Love God and love people.

Sounds great. Imagine what the world would look like if we, those of us who follow Jesus, would do that. We often think others should love us more or at least act more lovable. This is not what Jesus spoke of. He sets the model when He tells us that He first loved us. When? Well, of course, when we started acting right and going to church. Right? Wrong.

> But God showed his great love for us by
> sending Christ to die for us while we were
> still sinners.
>
> —ROMANS 5:8, NLT

So, we are to love those who show an interest in us
and are nice to us? No.

> You have heard that it was said, "You shall
> love your neighbor and hate your enemy."
> But I say to you, love your enemies, bless
> those who curse you, do good to those who
> hate you, and pray for those who spitefully
> use you and persecute you.
>
> —MATTHEW 5:43–44, NKJV

You see, we can always find a reason not to love
someone. I know a lot of great people, yet I can still
find something in them I don't like or don't agree
with. If I think this lets me off the hook, then I would
never have to love anyone.

Ever.

No one.

Obviously, that is wrong.

OK, we probably should define this word *love*. We use it so casually. "I love pizza," and "I love my kids and wife." Is it the same thing? When I speak of my love for my wife and kids, it suggests a lifelong commitment of frequent sacrificial acts on my part. But when I speak of my love for pizza, well, the pizza is the sacrifice. Seriously, there is no commitment to anything except to my plan to consume the pizza for my own benefit. As a matter of fact, if the pizza is poorly prepared or cold, my *love* diminishes to a mere *like* and maybe even to indifference or to not caring anything about the pizza. Too often, this is the way we love people. We love them for how they can benefit us, and if they don't meet our standards, our needs, or our expectations, then we no longer "love" them. In the Bible, is love such a fragile thing that it can be lost that easily? No, it isn't. The biblical concept of love is the love that drove Jesus to the cross.

> And here is how to measure it—the greatest love is shown when people lay down their lives for their friends.
>
> —JOHN 15:13, NLT

If we look at this idea only in terms of the literal crucifixion, we lose something. The crucifixion in

Scripture speaks of Jesus dying on the cross. But, you and I will probably never have to actually hang on a cross, so let's consider how the Cross applies to us. References to this idea pop up in many places, but let's look at the one above and at one other.

> We know what real love is because Christ gave up his life for us. And so we also ought to give up our lives for our Christian brothers and sisters.
>
> —1 JOHN 3:16, NLT

To love, to give up, to lie down—can you think of a less threatening stance to take? The image here is not of an arched back, a tense jaw, or clenched fists, but "to lie down." Someone who is lying down is not threatening. I would feel relaxed and at ease around someone who is in that position. Isn't that what love does? When we read the accounts of Jesus' life, we see people who were at ease in His presence.

Why?

They knew He loved them. John described himself as the disciple whom Jesus loved. It's interesting that no other disciple describes himself that way; only John does. John knew that Jesus loved him.

It has been said that in order to love others, we first

need to love ourselves. I strongly disagree, because the Bible never says that. Surely, if it were important enough, we would be told that. We are not. You have to really stretch a verse and twist its meaning to get that. No, the grace to love others begins with the realization that God first loved us. God loves you. Please say that out loud right now:

God loves me.

Stop. Say it again.

God loves me.

C'mon, say it out loud.

God loves me.

This is not just a verbal exercise. I mean think, really think, about that statement. *God loves me.* Why does God love me? The short answer is, I have no idea. I rejoice that He does, though. Did He wait for us to show promise or do something right before He loved us? No.

We love Him because He first loved us. (See 1 John 4:19, NKJV.)

So we find grace to love others as we increase in the understanding that God loves us.

Now we can love others.

Now we can always feel like loving others.

WHHHHHHHOOOOOAAA!!!

We won't always feel like loving others. If you have been married more than seven minutes, you have probably already felt like not loving your spouse. Love is not about feelings; it is about commitment. It is about loving someone even when you don't feel like it. How could we ever feel like loving our enemies as Jesus tells us to do?

> You have heard that it was said, "You shall love your neighbor and hate your enemy." But I say to you, love your enemies, bless those who curse you, do good to those who hate you, and pray for those who spitefully use you and persecute you.
> —MATTHEW 5:43–44, NKJV

You will seldom *feel* like loving your enemies. If you do, you are a much better person than I am. I feel like they should be judged and punished for their evil acts. My evil acts should fall under grace, but theirs should fall under judgment. That's convenient. No, loving people is an act of the will. And loving God is an act of the will as well. It's not that we don't feel like loving God, but sometimes in those dark moments when we think that God has forgotten us or we are unclear on God's plan for our life, we need to will to love God and to love others.

> You shall love the LORD your God with all your heart, with all your soul, and with all your strength.
> —DEUTERONOMY 6:5, NKJV

One of the translations of the word *soul* in the passage above is "will." This verse is part of the Shema. The Shema is Deuteronomy 6:4–9. The word *shema* is the first word in the passage, and translated literally, it means *hear* in Hebrew.

> Hear, O Israel: The LORD our God, the LORD is one! You shall love the LORD your God with all your heart, with all your soul, and with all your strength. And these words which I command you today shall

69

be in your heart. You shall teach them
diligently to your children, and shall talk
of them when you sit in your house, when
you walk by the way, when you lie down,
and when you rise up. You shall bind them
as a sign on your hand, and they shall be
as frontlets between your eyes. You shall
write them on the doorposts of your house
and on your gates.

—DEUTERONOMY 6:4–9, NKJV

The Jewish people do an interesting thing. They
take verse 9 literally. They write the verses (a rabbi
does) and place these verses in a *mezuzah*, which is
Hebrew for "doorpost." They then mount these mezu-
zahs on the doorways of their houses. Thereby, they
are constantly reminded to love God. Since the Bible
tells us we cannot love God without loving people,
it is also a reminder to love people. I think it is an
awesome thing to do to remind us of God's simple,
sweet truths.

Let's continue these thoughts on love by considering these verses:

Never seek revenge or bear a grudge against anyone, but love your neighbor as yourself. I am the LORD.

—LEVITICUS 19:18, NLT

Jesus replied, "'You must love the Lord your God with all your heart, all your soul, and all your mind.' This is the first and greatest commandment. A second is equally important: 'Love your neighbor as yourself.' All the other commandments and all the demands of the prophets are based on these two commandments."

—MATTHEW 22:37–40, NLT

These verses provide us with some very powerful tools to help us live a better life. How do they help? As you love people more, you will be loved more. It is simply impossible to love people more and not be loved more.

Want more love?

Give more love.

If you give, you will receive. Your gift will return to you in full measure, pressed down, shaken together to make room for more, and running over. Whatever measure you use in giving—large or small—it will be used to measure what is given back to you.

—LUKE 6:38, NLT

Love God

and love people,

because God first loved you.

eight

GET REAL

W E HAVE ALL heard that the church is filled with hypocrites. I sometimes quip, "Well, there is always room for one more." Some days run smoothly, and some days we don't do so great. That does not make us super-Christians on the good days and hypocritical on the bad days. If we begin to act like we never have bad days or never do bad things, then we begin moving down that steep slippery slope of hypocrisy. Jesus offered reassuring words for those who were caught in their sin but were longing for a better way. On the other hand, His words were not reassuring for those who were always pretending they had no problems.

I attended church for years before becoming a pastor. I am still intrigued by the way people interact at church. Churches have incredible potential to remind us of what is right and wrong in our lives and to encourage us. Yes, I know we already have that chapter covered. But sometimes churches can become a breeding ground for hypocrisy, a place where people are trying so hard to be *good* that they can't be *real* with one another. While we need to encourage each other to do what's right, we also need for people to understand that when we do wrong, we have a place to go. The church is supposed to be a hospital for sinners, not a museum for saints. So where is the problem? We have altar calls every Sunday for people to respond to the Holy Spirit's tugging on their hearts. Every Sunday some people respond, and every Sunday some people don't respond who should. They are hiding from God.

In church.

Bizarre, isn't it?

So, in the very place where we need to come clean, we don't. In the very place where we can tell God how we have messed up and need His help, we won't do it. Now, I have put some thought into this. In some ways I understand, especially in those churches that never give altar calls. An altar call is merely a call and an opportunity to respond to God. Sometimes I see people spell it *"alter* call," which I find interesting. The altar is a meeting place where we meet with God or worship Him. To be altered is to be changed. I like both; the two ideas fit together nicely. So, every week in church when we have an altar call we have the chance to get altered.

In modern times, we don't really have the chance to share our hearts, our struggles, and our problems with other people during altar calls. In times past, people could (and would) stand in a church service and testify about the problems they had been having and how God had seen them through it. We don't do that much anymore. Certainly, there was always potential with that practice for things to get messy in the middle of the service, but in many circles, especially in larger churches, it just doesn't work very well. What if everyone in a two thousand-member church got up each Sunday and shared his or her struggles?

So, does that mean our church services promote hypocrisy? Well, that's possible, but they also can be incredibly beautiful and meaningful. In addition to our large group meetings, we really need to add the intimacy and interaction that can only take place in small groups. At our church, we call them real life groups, and they are places where people can be real with one another about what is going on in their lives.

Keep in mind that God works in and through communities. God never told anyone just to go out to the desert and stay there and never interact with people again. He did tell people to go to the desert, but it was usually only for a season or for a journey. Then it would be time to come back and dwell in community again—or maybe sometimes to dwell together in the desert.

When we get to know people, something incredible happens. It is scary, but it is also beautiful. It is scary because we want to run as we realize how messed up we all are. We run because we don't want anyone to discover who we really are. It is beautiful because we begin to see we can be changed as we experience God in each other's lives. Like I was saying, it would be difficult logistically to go into a large church and, in the middle of service, begin to share where we are hurting, failing, or in need. It would probably be embarrassing, too. It's harder to feel that sense of intimacy and mutual trust among so many people. Large services are just not set up like that. But in a smaller group, we can and should share those things with one another.

Many of us would like to respond, "Well, I don't want to hear how messed up people are, and I don't want to tell anyone else how messed up I am." We would rather be detached from the realities of community. Years ago, groups of Christians decided that the problem was with everybody else, and they withdrew from the world. In parts of Greece, they built monasteries on top of steep cliffs. I wonder how long it was before they figured out that they had taken their problems with them.

Don't become hard-hearted about the problems of others, and don't become hard-hearted about your own problems. Small groups are not about seeing how messed up we are but actually about seeing first-hand how good God is, how He really is changing us if we will let Him. One of the most obvious places He is changing us is in the way we deal with each other. We can miss that in a large group setting. There are incredible things going on with amazing stories about what God is doing, but many times, we don't get to hear them. In a small group, you not only hear them, but you see them

and you touch them.

We live in a detached society. We exercise great control over our interactions. We did not get where we are overnight. There are great advantages with the way we communicate now. You can text, e-mail, or call someone who might be almost anywhere. You can also cut them off in mid-sentence and not even have to say good-bye. I am not saying I miss the days of speaking through tin cans with a string or yelling over the hills. I am saying, with the advantages come some tradeoffs. You see, when the Bible talks about the church, it speaks of it as a body, interconnected parts. All are different, but all share some things that are the same. We all look different and think different, but we also share many similarities—we all have faces, eyes, ears, arms, legs, etc. There was this TV show that was later made into a movie called *The Addams Family*. (This is not an endorsement of that show.) One of the characters was a disembodied hand that they called "Thing." It walked around on its fingers. I'm not sure how it ate. The absurdity of the idea was what made it humorous. Everyone understood it was not natural or normal; this was not the way the body was supposed to work.

That's right; it is not.

For someone to go to church and not be a part of the body, to be "disembodied" except for an hour or two on Sunday morning, is not natural or normal and certainly not what God intended. We need to see that sort of Christianity as abnormal and look for what God intended, a community of people in relationship with one another, a place where everybody knows your name.

Is it scary? Yes, it can be. It is also an incredible opportunity to see God up close, doing something in someone's life. To see a life changed is glorious. Be careful, the life you see changed right before your eyes might be your own.

Quit hiding in church.

Get real.

Join a small group.

nine

GET DOING

MANY PEOPLE DIE with unrealized dreams. They were going to do this or they were going to do that. Many Christians will die never having really served the Lord. Oh, they've been taught about it, they've heard about it, and they may have even felt like they should do something. But they never do.

Days slip into weeks, weeks into months, months into years, and years into a lifetime. Before you know it, your opportunities are all behind you. Jesus is inviting you to join Him in an incredible adventure. You can be a spectator, watching people change the world, or you can join them. I've heard many excuses for not getting involved, but I've never heard a good reason. Let's look at some common excuses:

I don't have time.

Well this is a truth—sort of. You don't. You can't store time. You can't create time. You can't save it for later like restaurant leftovers that you take home in a "doggy bag." When you spend your time on something, you can't get a refund; it's done. Be careful what you spend it on. Here is the problem with this often-used excuse. Every day and every week there are thousands of people who *make* the time to become involved in their local church. Just showing up on Sunday morning does not constitute getting involved. I'm talking about serving.

- Helping clean the church
- Caring for children
- Greeting people
- Folding bulletins
- Things that we can all do

No one can do everything, but all can do some things.

So the people who do these things, do they have more time than the rest of us? Do they get twenty-five or twenty-six hours in a day? No, they make serving a priority; they decide to set time aside for that purpose. The interesting thing is, the things that occupy us—our work, our meetings, some of our social activities—do not really fulfill or satisfy us. Showing a house, selling a car, entering data, and landscaping a yard can be good things. There is just not that soul-satisfying experience of touching another human being, of somehow helping them and making their life better. Helping others produces in us a spiritual sense of fulfillment. I think some people search for corporate power when they are really looking for the power to change a life. You have the time. You may choose not to serve God by serving others, but that's your choice. You do have the time. If you don't make the time now, you may have a long time to regret your decision later.

I don't agree with everything going on in this church.

That's a classic excuse. But if you wait until you find a church where you agree with everything they do, you'll probably never know the joy of experiencing God's heart by serving others. That excuse allows us to completely ignore that Jesus calls us to serve. If we are not following Him into service, we need to ask ourselves, Are we really following Him? Consider these passages:

> If any man serve me, let him follow me;
> and where I am, there shall also my

servant be: if any man serve me, him will
my Father honour.

—JOHN 12:26, KJV

For, brethren, ye have been called unto
liberty; only use not liberty for an occa-
sion to the flesh, but by love serve one
another.

—GALATIANS 5:13, KJV

Friend, if you are waiting to find a church where
you agree with everything they do before involving
yourself in service, guess what? You will always have
an excuse to not serve.

You are off the hook forever.

Or are you?

In the Book of Acts, the early church experienced
many disagreements. There were disagreements
regarding the keeping of the Law (the observation
of the rite of circumcision, for example), eating meat
sacrificed to idols, sharing bread with Gentiles, and
on and on. Some have been recorded, and I am sure
many of their disagreements were not recorded.

However, they served alongside one another and saw incredible things happen.

☙

The Bible is filled with God interrupting the lives of people. God interrupted Moses with a burning bush. He interrupted the shepherd boy David with a call to be king. He interrupted some fishermen with a call to change the world. He interrupted a religious leader, Paul, with a call to go tell the world the good news. God is still interrupting lives—my life, your life. He wants to interrupt our lives and replace our plans with His plans. He wants to take our selfish, self-absorbed lives and transform them into incredibly blessed lives, lives that will bless God and others.

Could it be that God wants to interrupt your busy life with something much deeper, more meaningful, spiritually powerful and eternally rewarding? Oh, I forgot.

You're

too

busy.

Spinning around in circles.

Even if you win the rat race, that only makes you head rat.

Friend, this is one of the keys to a better life. Realize that your life is not your own until you give it away. If you try to hold on to it, you will lose it.

Forever.

If you give it away, you will gain it.

Forever.

> For whoever desires to save his life will lose it, but whoever loses his life for My sake will find it.
> —MATTHEW 16:25, NKJV

The church, from its beginning, was made to be something that was mainly powered by volunteers, not by a few elite, hired specialists. In our church we have 130 people who care for our smaller children. Imagine what that same ministry would look like if the two paid staff members were the only ones caring for them.

> He said to his disciples, "The harvest is
> so great, but the workers are so few. So
> pray to the Lord who is in charge of the
> harvest; ask him to send out more workers
> for his fields."
>
> —MATTHEW 9:37–38, NLT

It would be sad if the harvest Jesus was talking about were merely about flowers or even food. It is the ultimate human joy (and tragedy) that He is talking about souls. Jesus is telling us that after all He did to redeem us we still need to choose to be involved.

The followers of Jesus will never do all they can until they begin to do all they can.

The church will never reach all it can reach until all those it has already reached begin to join in the cause.

Think of it, Jesus lifted both hands as He died on the cross for us. How can it be that there are those who say they follow Him but won't lift one hand to help?

> Dear brothers and sisters, what's the use
> of saying you have faith if you don't prove
> it by your actions? That kind of faith can't
> save anyone.
>
> —JAMES 2:14, NLT

Fool! When will you ever learn that faith that does not result in good deeds is useless?

—JAMES 2:20, NLT

Just as the body is dead without a spirit, so also faith is dead without good deeds.

—JAMES 2:26, NLT

For your faith to be alive it has to be active, moving, and blessing others. The reality is, you cannot live a selfish life and live a blessed life, too. It may be a life filled with things, but it will not be a thing filled with life.

EPILOGUE

(Or, "Things I Forgot to Say")

THERE WILL BE two kinds of folks who look this book over. One kind will read it and say, "This is absurd. I don't completely understand how this can help, so obviously it can't." Friend, over the years, I've made many visits to the doctor when I got sick. I have never fully understood the medicines they prescribed; but, I took them, and I got better. My ability to understand the diagnosis or how the prescription worked made no difference in the healing process. It was not my understanding but my response to the doctor's advice that helped make me better. Your response to this book really can help—or your lack of response will keep it from helping.

The principles in this book are derived from the Bible, and they operate the same way. The benefit comes not just from reading, but in doing. Make some changes. Do some of the things mentioned.

Watch how small choices really can make big changes in your life.

Maybe you think these answers are too easy, that life is much more complicated than this.

Well, life certainly can get complicated, but the answers are usually simple and easily understood.

I spoke of "two kinds of folks." The other group of folks will respond to this book and do what it says. Books don't often come with a guarantee, but this one does. The guarantee is based upon the promise of Jesus. If we do these things we will find life, an abundant life, a satisfied life, a meaningful life, a better life.

Perhaps you are already doing some of the things I've mentioned, but not others. Start from the beginning and do them one by one. Try reading back over a chapter until you really start to do the things it suggests.

Maybe you are doing most of these things already, but your attitude or passion has begun to slip. May God rekindle your flame, friend. There is a cold, dark world out there that needs to see what a blessed life looks like.

May your life be a reflection of God's light. May we join together as we light up the world with He who is the light of our soul.

Thank you so much for reading this book. It is my prayer that it will change your life and that you will never be the same again. If I can help you in any way along your spiritual journey, please let me know. It is my honor to walk the path with you.

NOTES

CHAPTER 4
BE THE CHURCH—LEARN ABOUT
GOD AND THE BIBLE

1. Robert Chapman, quoted in Erwin W. Lutzer, *Seven Reasons Why You Can Trust the Bible* (Chicago, IL: Moody Publishing, 1998).

2. Mark Twain, quoted in John R. W. Stott, *Christ the Liberator* (Downers Grove, IL: InterVarsity Press, 1971), 214.

CHAPTER 5
BE THE CHURCH—LIVE FOR GOD

1. Corrie ten Boom, with John and Elizabeth Sherrill, *The Hiding Place* (New York City, NY: Chosen Books, 1971).

CHAPTER 6
BE THE CHURCH—GIVE TO GOD
THROUGH THE CHURCH

1. "Christians worldwide had personal income totaling more than $16 trillion in 2007 but gave only 2 percent, or $370 billion, to Christian causes" (David B. Barrett, Tom M. Johnson, Peter F. Crossing, "Missiometrics: Creating Your Own Analysis of Global

Data," International Bulletin of Missionary Research Vol. 31, No. 1, 2007, 8). "Donating Over Tithing: Overall, only 3 to 5 percent of those who donate money to a church tithe (give 10 percent of) their incomes" (George Barna, How to Increase Giving in Your Church: A Practical Guide to the Sensitive Task of Raising Money for Your Church or Ministry [Ventura, CA: Regal Books, 1997], 20). "Tithing: 9 Percent of American 'born-again' adults tithed in 2004" (The Barna Group, Ltd., "Americans Donate Billions to Charity, But Giving to Churches Has Declined," April 25, 2005, http://www.barna.org). "Then and Now: Giving by North American churchgoers was higher during the Great Depression (3.3 percent of per capita income in 1933) than it was after a half-century of unprecedented prosperity (2.5 percent in 2004)" (John Ronsvalle and Sylvia Ronsvalle, *The State of Church Giving Through 2004: Will We Will? 16th ed.* [Champaign, IL: Empty Tomb, 2006], 36).

ABOUT the AUTHOR

DAVID MCGEE HAS led an interesting life. He was born a deaf-mute. Doctors discovered that he was 95 percent deaf and that his tongue was attached in front of his lower teeth. At five years old, he could not speak. Miraculously, this was corrected through nine surgeries and four years of speech therapy. David lived as a professional rock musician, a remodeling company owner, a recording studio owner, and a traveling Christian teacher/musician. Now he is the senior pastor of a growing fellowship. His story is certainly a unique and exciting one.

Seven years ago, David moved his home Bible study into the public sphere. That once-small fellowship of fifteen people has grown to over two thousand in weekly attendance. He has since launched a satellite church and plans to launch several more. David's teachings are broadcast around the world on TV, radio, and the Internet in an ever-increasing market. David has appeared on numerous television and radio shows, making appearances on ABC, CBS, CBN, FOX, NBC, and TBN.

His verse-by-verse teaching through the Bible is marked by powerful personal insights, humorous comments, and in-depth knowledge of the Hebrew language and custom. This style of teaching deeply impacts the lives of those who come in contact with David and his ministry. One of the things that makes this ministry so unique is David's love for God, for people, and for the Bible. In a time when biblical literacy has fallen to an all-time low, David makes the Bible fun, exciting, and personally meaningful. With his rock-star image, he is seen as cutting edge and culturally relevant, yet biblically solid.

He has a deep respect for the Jewish roots of Christianity, demonstrated by his leading numerous and extensive trips to Israel, leading Passovers, and use of the Hebrew language to tie the Old Testament and the New Testament together in a powerful and unique way. It is the passion of this man and this ministry to communicate the timeless truths of the Bible to a lost, dying, and confused world.

In addition to exploding media attention and increasing DVD and CD sales, David has expanded his ministry team. He has released his first book, *Cross the Bridge to Life*, David has begun to speak at large-scale events, including an outreach in South Miami Beach during spring break.

> And they were astonished beyond measure, saying, "He has done all things well. He makes both the deaf to hear and the mute to speak."
>
> —Mark 7:37, NKJV

For more on David McGee's testimony, visit davidmcgee.org

FREE DAILY E-VOTIONALS

Sign up for my daily devotional thoughts (e-votionals) and periodic updates at:

www.crossthebridge.com
or
www.davidmcgee.org

Treat yourself to captivating devotions overflowing with relevant wisdom, inspiration, power, and hope! You will find encouragement daily with my e-votionals. Join the thousands who have already discovered intimacy with Jesus and strengthened faith with these daily e-votionals. Incorporate them in your family devotions or enjoy them as personal quiet times with God.

These e-votionals can be used as a great way to encourage anyone to devote daily time with God. All it takes is a moment!

PASTOR DAVID MCGEE

crossthebridge

Think about life. Think about Jesus.

CROSS the BRIDGE
OUTREACH MINISTRIES

You're invited to partner with Cross the Bridge Outreach Ministries to bring large-scale events, TV, radio, and Internet into the lives of those who have not received Jesus as Lord and Savior. Help us to equip people to cross the bridge from death to life and from spectator Christianity to a life dedicated to serving the Lord.

Visit www.crossthebridge.com to find valuable information, such as:

- Archives of Pastor David's radio program and teaching. You will also find a listing of broadcasting stations and times.
- Information about events in your area
- Daily e-votionals
- A "How to Grow in God" section to encourage your daily walk with God

- Downloads of audio and video
  messages

You will also find a link to Pastor David's home church, Calvary Chapel of the Triad, in Kernersville, North Carolina. Please visit www.davidmcgee.org, where you will learn more information about Pastor David and the church. There, you can check out our online bookstore.

Or, call toll-free:

1-877-458-5508

Cross the Bridge Outreach Ministries
P.O. Box 2288
Kernersville, NC 27284

www.crossthebridge.com

FOR MORE RESOURCES
by DAVID MCGEE

In appreciation of your support of this life-changing ministry by buying this book, we'd like to bless you with a 10 percent discount code (see bottom of next page), good on all items in our eStore at www.cross-thebridge.com. Please visit the site often because we are always adding new ways to help you in your adventure.

Passover Seder

David McGee guides you through nearly three hours of the Passover Seder meal, revealing the prophetic significance and fulfillment of each step in the process. Every believer in Jesus must experience this special DVD teaching! Retail: $19.99 Your Cost: $17.99 (with discount code)

Israel: The Bible and You

Join David McGee as he takes you through the Bible to discover the prophetic significance of the feasts on this DVD. Retail: $14.99 Your Cost: $13.49 (with discount code)

Israel: The Journey Home

David McGee leads us through fifteen actual sites in Israel, unlocking the Scriptures in the Holy Land. Enjoy the rich history of Israel on this three DVD set. Retail: $29.99 Your Cost: $26.99 (with discount code)

All for One

Enjoy this enthusiastic contemporary worship CD recorded by David McGee and the Calvary Chapel of the Triad worship team. Includes five of David's original compositions! Retail: $14.99 Your Cost: $13.49 (with discount code)

MP3 of Romans

David McGee teaches through the Book of Romans, covering each verse with incredible biblical and historical insight. With his vast knowledge and personal insight, David provides practical application for our daily lives in every teaching. Retail: $29.99 Your Cost: $26.99 (with discount code)

All prices effective as of the date of publication
Subject to change without notice

CTBL2Life1
10% off